Straight to the Source

Books

John Hamilton

ABDO
Publishing Company

visit us at
www.abdopub.com

Published by ABDO Publishing Company, 4940 Viking Drive, Edina, Minnesota 55435.
Copyright © 2005 by Abdo Consulting Group, Inc. International copyrights reserved in all
countries. No part of this book may be reproduced in any form without written permission from
the publisher. The Checkerboard Library™ is a trademark and logo of ABDO Publishing
Company.

Printed in the United States.

Cover Photo: Corbis
Interior Photos: Corbis pp. 1, 5, 6, 7, 8, 9, 11, 14, 15, 25, 27, 28; PhotoEdit p. 17

Series Coordinator: Stephanie Hedlund
Editors: Heidi M. Dahmes, Megan Murphy
Art Direction: Neil Klinepier

Library of Congress Cataloging-in-Publication Data

Hamilton, John, 1959-
    Books / John Hamilton.
        p. cm. -- (Straight to the source)
    Includes index.
    Summary: An introduction to the history, printing, and production of books.
    ISBN 1-59197-543-3
    1. Books--Juvenile literature. 2. Printing--Juvenile literature. [1. Books. 2. Printing.] I. Title.

Z116.A2H29 2004
002--dc22
                                                                            2003061677

Contents

Books

Before there were books, people had to relay information orally. Parents and grandparents would teach their children stories. Then in prehistoric times, people began drawing on cave walls and animal skins. They used burned sticks and soft rocks as their pens.

These early drawings were the beginning of the written word. **Pictographs** led to alphabets that were carved on **tablets** and eventually written in books. Today, books pass on information. They also entertain and teach those who read them.

There are many kinds of books. Books of fiction are based on an author's imagination, while nonfiction books are based on facts. Textbooks and scholarly books are also available.

Books are sources of information. Some can support an argument in a research paper. So, finding and using books are important parts of a student's career.

Opposite page: *Reference books are good resources for research papers.*

Early Books

The first books were made to store records. These records were written on clay or wax **tablets**. In 2500 BC, Egyptians moved away from the use of tablets. They began writing on papyrus reeds.

In order to write on papyrus, the Egyptians laid strips of the plant side by side. Then, they crossed more strips over the top. Finally, they covered all the strips with a paste.

Clay tablets may have been produced as early as 3100 BC.

When the sheets were dry, the Egyptians wrote on one side of them. These long sheets were then rolled up and stored in temples. The Greeks adopted the papyrus rolls and passed them on to the Romans. The Romans called them *volumen*, which is Latin for "book."

The first book as we know it appeared around AD 400. By this time, people had begun to write more,

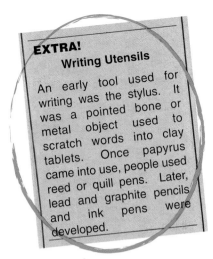

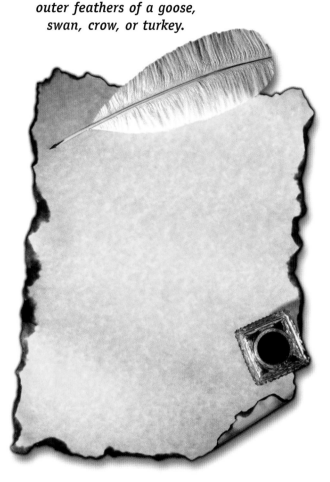

Quills were taken from the outer feathers of a goose, swan, crow, or turkey.

and the scrolls became difficult to use. So, they folded the papyrus into piles of pages. They stitched one side and created what was called a codex.

Soon, papyrus codices were replaced by ones made of leather, **parchment**, or vellum. These materials were all made from stretched sheepskins, calfskins, or goatskins. People could write on both sides of these surfaces.

During the **Middle Ages**, monks copied codices for their churches. Beautiful gold pictures and patterns were added to the codices. These decorations were called **manuscript** illuminations.

In the 1100s, book production moved from monasteries to universities. These universities had developed in France, Italy, and England, causing more people to read. However, a single document could not be used by several people at once.

The universities created new jobs such as stationers, or book copiers. When students needed a book for a class, they could go to the stationer. There, the students could copy the book by hand. Or, they could pay the book copier to produce the book for them.

Many scrolls also contained manuscript illuminations.

By 1151, paper had slowly made its way to Europe from China. Europeans learned how to make **pulp** from rags, chips of

Vellum was a delicate parchment made from the processed skins of the young of cows, goats, and sheep.

bark, and water. This material was pressed to make a strong paper, which eventually replaced vellum.

Over time, more people wanted books. It became difficult for stationers to keep up. They needed a quick way to make many books at once.

EXTRA!

Papermaking

The first-known paper was invented in China by a man named Ts'ai Lun in AD 105. Chinese prisoners showed people in Samarqand the papermaking process in 751.

In 1151, the first paper in Europe was made in Spain. Paper mills then rapidly spread throughout Europe.

Early Printing

Printing developed because of the need for multiple copies of books. Block printing was the first-known printing method. In the 500s, pages of words and pictures were carved in reverse and then printed.

In 868, the earliest-known block-printed book, *Diamond Sutra*, was made in China. Even with block printing, books could not be made fast enough. In about 1041, Chinese printer Pi Sheng invented **movable type**.

Movable type did not arrive in Europe for nearly 400 years. Around 1440, Johannes Gutenberg figured out a way to make single letters out of metal.

Gutenberg lined the metal letters in a tray and covered them with ink. After he pressed paper onto them, he could move the letters to form the next page. In 1455, he made the first printed Bible, now known as the Gutenberg Bible.

Opposite page: In the early 1400s, a Dutchman named Laurens Janszoon Coster began making wooden block letters. Soon, durable metal letters were created.

Following Gutenberg's success, other people began printing books. Soon, they wanted to add pictures to the words. In 1461, pictures were cut into wood, inked, and pressed onto paper. These were called woodcuts or wood engravings.

Around 1500, people started to demand color in their books. This led to **manuscript** illumination by hand. Eventually, printers began using colored inks on their presses. In 1719, Jacques-Christophe Le Blond filed a patent to print with blue, yellow, red, and black inks.

Le Blond would print all the sheets in one color and then clean the press. Next, he ran the same pieces of paper through the press with another color. This time-consuming process was done for each new color. So, early books had little color.

In the 1800s, technology made printing easier. At this time, machines began making paper. Previously, paper had been made by hand and was hard to obtain.

Then, cloth covers replaced expensive leather covers. Color printing took less time, too. So, books became more affordable. Soon, more people began buying and reading books.

Over time, printing standards have developed and improved. Today, a small publisher may put out only one book title a year. A large publisher, however, is able to print and sell hundreds of different titles.

Today, printing with four colors is common. Many newspapers, magazines, and books have full-color images.

Today's Books

Today, people enjoy reading about a variety of subjects. Because of this, books are divided into five main categories.

The first category of books is general interest, or trade. Trade books include all novels, picture books, poetry, and other fiction. Nonfiction, such as biographies, music, and how-to books, are also in this category.

Another type of book is a textbook. Textbooks are used for instruction. They are developed especially for their audience. Most subjects that you study at school have textbooks.

Scholarly books make up a third category. These books are written for specific professions by scholars of that

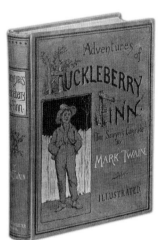

The Adventures of Huckleberry Finn
is an example of a trade book.

field. Religious books form a fourth category. They often contain history or philosophy of a religion.

A final type of book is the reference book. This category includes encyclopedias, atlases, and dictionaries. Reference books are used to verify facts. They are good sources for research papers.

There are textbooks to help students learn about nearly every subject.

Bookmaking

Producing a book is a complex project. The process begins with an idea for a **manuscript**. Sometimes, a publisher develops an idea and asks an author to write about it. Other times, an author develops his or her own idea.

After an author writes a story, he or she sends it to a publisher. An author may submit an **unsolicited** manuscript. Or, a **literary agent** submits it.

Once a manuscript is accepted, several editors look it over. These people check spelling, facts, and style to make sure the book is ready for printing. They often work with an author to produce the best book possible.

After it is edited, a manuscript goes to **prepress**. At this stage, layout issues are decided. First, photographs or illustrations are chosen for the book. Then, all the words must be typed into an electronic computer file. This is called typesetting.

A book may be designed at the publishing house. However, book packagers are freelance companies that also lay out books.

After typesetting, a book is designed by a layout artist. During this stage, a **typeface** is chosen. Once the type and images are all laid out, each page of the book is proofread for errors. Finally, it's time to start the printing process.

Ready to Print

When a book is ready for printing, there are several types of presses to choose from. Deciding the kind of press to use is based on many things. These include the number of colors, pages, and books being printed.

One type of printing is letterpress, which is based on the relief method. In this method, words or images are raised. Ink is applied to this raised area. Then, a piece of paper is pressed onto it. The raised area is printed onto the paper.

A second type of press is the offset press. Offset printing is based on the fact that ink and water don't mix. The words and pictures on a page are put onto a thin **aluminum**, steel, or plastic plate with a greasy pencil or ink.

The **printing plate** is wrapped around a printing **cylinder**. First water and then the printing ink are applied to the plate. The printing ink adheres, or sticks, to the places that have letters or photos. The water keeps ink away from the rest of the page.

Next, the **printing plate** transfers the images onto a soft rubber "blanket." From the blanket, the image is printed onto paper. Because pages are not printed directly from the plate, this process is called offset lithography.

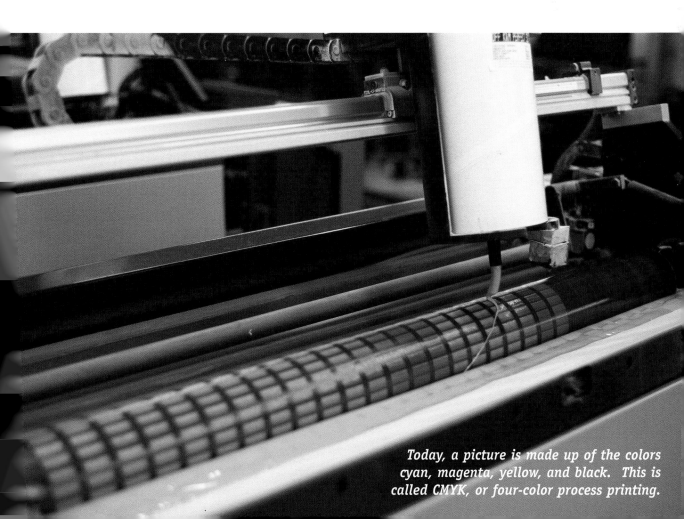

Today, a picture is made up of the colors cyan, magenta, yellow, and black. This is called CMYK, or four-color process printing.

For either press, there are two ways paper is fed to the machines. Slower presses are sheetfed, so one sheet is printed at a time. The web press uses giant rolls of paper. This allows printing and folding to be done in one fast, continuous process.

Once a press is chosen, the **prepress** team develops a book's **printing plates**. Each plate will print a number of pages on a single section of paper called a signature. When a signature is folded, the pages appear in order.

Signatures may have 4 to 64 pages. Prepress workers use the book's height, width, and page number to determine the number of folds in a signature. This, in turn, tells them how many signatures are in a book and how many plates to make.

After the signatures are printed, a machine folds them. Then, a gathering machine places them in the correct page order. Once all of the signatures are assembled, another machine cuts the edges. You now have the book's pages.

A book's pages are proofread several times during the printing process. One proof includes making sure the signature is laid out in the correct order.

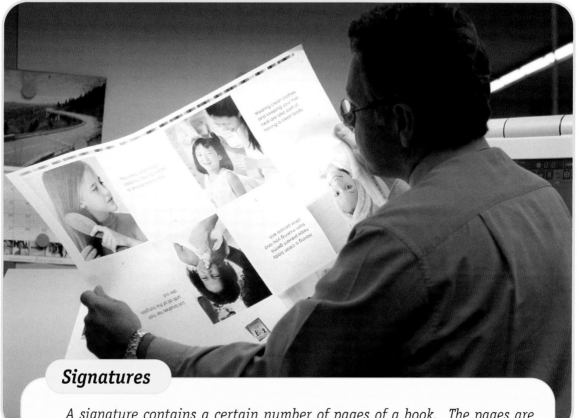

Signatures

A signature contains a certain number of pages of a book. The pages are laid out so that when a signature is folded into smaller squares, the pages are in the correct order. All signatures must have a multiple of four pages. There are several different names for signatures.

◆ Folio - By folding a signature in the middle, you make 2 leaves. When you count the front and back of each leaf, you have 4 pages.
◆ Quarto - By folding a signature twice, you have 4 leaves or 8 pages.
◆ Octavo - Folding four times produces 8 leaves or 16 pages. This is also called an eightvo.
◆ Duodecimo - A single page folded into 12 leaves makes 24 pages.

Binding

After the signatures are cut, the pages go to the binder. There, they are joined together. Pages are bound in several ways.

One type of binding is side sewing. In a side-sewn book, holes are drilled through one side of the pages, creating the spine. Then, the pages are stitched together.

Some books are held together by perfect binding. In this method, the pages are glued together, instead of sewn. Usually, perfect-bound books are not as sturdy as side-sewn books.

After a book is bound, a protective cover is placed on it. Today, books may have hard or soft covers. A hardcover is sturdy cardboard that is covered in cloth, leather, or vinyl. A softcover is made of heavy paper. Once a book is covered, it is ready to be shipped.

EXTRA!

Early Bookbinding

The earliest books had their pages sewn together. The monks sewed the vellum pages of a book by hand. This was called hand binding.

After hand binding was completed, the book's outside pages were glued to wooden boards. Next, the boards were covered in decorated leather. Finally, the book was closed with a metal clasp.

At the side-sewing machine, holes are drilled into a book's signatures. The pages are then sewn together with a strong nylon or cotton thread.

Inside a Book

Completed books may look very different from each other. However, there are several features that are the same for most books.

The first feature is the title page. This page appears on page one of a book. It provides the book's title, author, and publisher information.

Another feature is the copyright page. It is found on page two, and it tells readers who has the right to print the book. It includes the publisher's information and the year the book was published.

The copyright page contains the Library of Congress (LOC) Cataloging-in-Publication (CIP) data, too. This includes information about the author, as well as important cataloging numbers. It often provides a short summary of the book, too.

The copyright and contents pages of this book

visit us at
www.abdopub.com

Published by ABDO Publishing Company, 4940 Viking Drive, Edina, Minnesota 55435.
Copyright © 2005 by Abdo Consulting Group, Inc. International copyrights reserved in all countries. No part of this book may be reproduced in any form without written permission from the publisher. The Checkerboard Library™ is a trademark and logo of ABDO Publishing Company.

Printed in the United States.

Cover Photo: Corbis
Interior Photos: Corbis pp. 1, 5, 6, 7, 8, 9, 11, 14, 15, 23, 27, 28; Photo Edit p. 17

Series Coordinator: Stephanie Hedlund
Editors: Heidi Dahmes, Megan Murphy
Art Direction: Neil Klinepier

Library of Congress Cataloging-in-Publication Data

Hamilton, John, 1959-
   Books / John Hamilton.
      p. cm. -- (Straight to the source)
   Includes index.
   Summary: An introduction to the history, printing, and production of books.
   ISBN 1-59197-543-3
   1. Books--Juvenile literature. 2. Printing--Juvenile literature. [1. Books. Printing.] I. Title.

Z116.A2H29 2004
002--dc22
                                                        2003046677

Contents

The table of contents is a common feature of nonfiction books. It is found on page three of this book. It shows a reader each chapter and the page that it starts on. It is one way to quickly locate information.

Most reference books include an index on the last pages. An index provides an alphabetical list of important names, places, and subjects. It then gives page numbers that contain that information. This makes the information easy to find in the text.

EXTRA!

Cataloging Numbers

The Library of Congress CIP data contains several pieces of information. This data helps librarians and bookstores know what is in the book.

One item is the International Standard Book Number (ISBN). For more than 30 years, each book around the world has been given an individual ISBN.

The CIP data tells what type of book it is. Every book fits into a specific category, which makes it easier to be stored and then found on library shelves.

There are other features that help people find information. One is thumb tabs, which help you find information in a book that is arranged alphabetically.

Finding Books

Books may be sold to many places. Bookstores buy books and then sell them to the public. Libraries also buy them. You can even buy e-books, or electronic books, on the Internet.

Libraries have thousands, sometimes millions, of books. Because of this, libraries needed to develop a way to sort them. Over time, two methods have evolved.

In 1876, librarian Melvil Dewey designed a way to sort books. He called it the Dewey decimal classification system. Dewey put every book into one of ten numbered categories. Each of these main categories was divided into 100 subdivisions.

In the early 1900s, the LOC developed its own classification method. It has 21 categories. Each category is further divided by numbers. LOC classification is used in research and university systems.

Each book is assigned a Dewey decimal and LOC number. To locate an item in a library's **archives**, you will search its catalog. The catalog will provide a list of books and their classification numbers. This will lead you to a book's place on the shelf.

The library has a system to keep track of its items. So before you leave the library, you must check out your items.

Book Citation

When writing a research paper, you will use books to get information. But, just because a book is published doesn't mean it is **accurate**. So before you write your paper, you have to **evaluate** your sources.

Once you have found reliable sources, you can start writing your paper. It is important to write your work in your own words. If you use the exact words of another author as your own, you are plagiarizing.

A research paper needs facts to support your opinion. Books are good places to find the facts you need!

Plagiarizing is like stealing. So, take careful notes when gathering information. Then paraphrase, which means to write the information in your own words. Even after paraphrasing, you still have to give credit to the original author. This is called citing a source.

Citation lets your readers know where to look for more information on your topic. There are many ways to cite a source. The most common is Modern Language Association (MLA) style. The MLA handbook or a librarian can help you cite sources.

EXTRA!

MLA Citation

MLA style requires three pieces of information for citing books. First, cite the author's name. Next, include the title of the book. Finally, insert the publisher information, which is the publisher's location, name, and the date of publication.

Krensky, Stephen. Breaking Into Print. New York: Little, 1996.

Books help people learn and pass on information. Newspapers and magazines also do these things. But, they are often thrown away. Books are more permanent. So, it is important to preserve them for future generations.

Glossary

accurate - free of errors. Something with errors is inaccurate.

aluminum - a light, soft, metallic element that is used in making machinery and other products.

archives - organized records.

cylinder - a solid figure of two parallel circles bound by a curved surface. A soda can is an example of a cylinder.

evaluate - to determine the meaning or importance of something.

literary agent - a person who represents an author.

manuscript - a book or article written by hand or typed before being published.

Middle Ages - a period from about AD 500 to 1500 characterized by a lack of education, the loss of artistic and technical skills, population decrease, and primitive economic life.

movable type - a rectangular block that contains a letter or symbol for printing. It can be moved or rearranged to produce different pages.

parchment - refined leather that is prepared so it can be written on.

pictograph - a picture that represents a word or idea.

prepress - before printing.

printing plate - a cast or mold of a page of type to be printed.

pulp - a soft, moist material prepared from various fibers, such as wood or rags. Pulp is used to make paper.

tablet - a thin, flat slab of wood or stone that is used for writing or drawing.

typeface - a style of type.

unsolicited - something that is not requested.

codex - KOH-dehks

papyrus - puh-PEYE-ruhs

Pi Sheng - BEE SHUHNG

plagiarism - PLAY-juh-rih-zuhm

unsolicited - uhn-suh-LIH-suht-ehd

To learn more about books, visit ABDO Publishing Company on the World Wide Web at **www.abdopub.com**. Web sites about books are featured on our Book Links page. These links are routinely monitored and updated to provide the most current information available.

Index